magnified

ALSO BY MINNIE BRUCE PRATT

MINNIE BRUCE PRATT

WESLEYAN POETRY

magnified

Wesleyan University Press   Middletown, Connecticut

Wesleyan University Press
Middletown CT 06459
www.wesleyan.edu/wespress
© 2021 Minnie Bruce Pratt
All rights reserved
Manufactured in the United States of America
Designed by Mindy Basinger Hill
Typeset in Adobe Jenson Pro

Names: Pratt, Minnie Bruce, author.
Title: Magnified / Minnie Bruce Pratt.
Description: Middletown, Connecticut : Wesleyan
    University Press, [2021] |
Series: Wesleyan poetry | Includes index. |
    Summary: "Chronicling one year in the life
    of a queer couple facing life-threatening
    illness, this sequence of poems explores what
    words can do to hold off loss and death while
    living on in a world of injustice and sorrow"—
    Provided by publisher.
Identifiers: LCCN 2020044854 (print)
    LCCN 2020044855 (ebook)
    ISBN 9780819580054 (cloth)
    ISBN 9780819580061 (trade paperback)
    ISBN 9780819580078 (ebook)
Subjects: LCGFT: Poetry.
Classification: LCC PS3566.R35 M34 2021 (print)
    | LCC PS3566.R35 (ebook) | DDC 811/.54—
    dc23
LC record available at
    https://lccn.loc.gov/2020044854
LC ebook record available at
    https://lccn.loc.gov/2020044855

5   4   3   2   1

In memoriam **LESLIE FEINBERG**

CONTENTS

. . . hourglass

Someone sang, *Oh death! Oh death! Won't you*
pass me over for another day? Someone said, *I*

dreamed of you last night. I dreamed you
were telling me your whole life story.

Whole. Whorled. Welkin, winkle, wrinkle.
The loop of time holds us all together.

The pile of laundry on the bed. You
folding socks one inside the other. We
have had this day, and now this night.

The clothes are put away, and from the bed we see
the moon folding light into darkness, not death.

3

BLUE MOON

The trees creak overhead, squeaky doors pushed forth
and back in the wind. On the porch we watch the moon
rising from whisper to guess to peach, white, then blue.

Once in a blue moon a love like this comes along.
We weren't standing alone. Lots of people, a room vast
with politics and that ex-lover playing catch-my-eye.

You read us a story, the one who had been you. A past,
the one who had been me. Your torn shirt, my needle's eye.

We had been alone. We had read what the other had asked.
The light shone on the pages, your face up-tilted in the glare.
Glory, mirror, future. Later I knew you were looking up at me.

I knew you, you knew me. We looked at each other,
shining on each other. Shining-on sun. Sailing-on moon.

4

That spring you and I leaned over the edge,
staring into the swamp. What was in there?
Amphibian eyes glinting like treasure in the water,
gold dots of pollen flecking a sodden carpet.

That spring we saw you were beginning to die.
The arrowhead leaves flew slowly up green
out of the murky water. You got sick and sicker.   5

We leaned. Our shadows reached into the water.
We looked down into the mud, past where we'd seen,
to where what-could-be lived, waiting to come.

I type out *life expectancy* onto the keyboard.

The end is never definite, so we drove to the lake
and walked into the impending storm. I don't want
to rush this part. We were very happy, the huge
warm breath of west wind damp on our faces.

And then we sat in the car and held hands
while the rain shook its silver tasseled grass.

But this morning, your gaunt sleeping face,
the line of your body disappearing into the bed.

When I step out the door to go to work, I'm in
the hallway of a future without you. When I go
to get morning coffee what I drink is grief,
and at the bottom of the paper cup is loneliness.

Light dawns quickly on the computer screen.
You play me a song before I go off to work.

The song sings: *Not there, not there anymore.*
The people we were, there, are gone forever.

What we are not now: Not urban dancers,
not the couple practicing our perverse moves
in the black-and-white diner aisle, not the us
scrambling like rain through police barricades
in Times Square, not the me clasping white roses
escaped through an iron fence in the Village.

Goodbye, goodbye, the ones I've loved.
So long, our last life fading, video ending.

Behind us the rising sun casts its red stare
upon our wall. The shadow of what is here.

Lamp, leaf, bird. But not us, not yet.
Even though we are ready, and up so early.

7

At twilight, in the fold of this day's pall,
you lift the bed covers up, and I climb in.

The bed is a cave, the sheets cool as stone.
The bed is a nest we fold flesh into, belly
to back, knee to knee-fold, wrist-bone to hand.

8

Our ribs brace the bed, a boat to carry us into,
through, the little death that lives in every night.

I wake again at three a.m. Our cardboard boxes
sit unpacked in every room. Taxes, losses, old
dishes, death. But you still breathe beside me.

If I can put each thing into its place, there will be
a place for the boat to land where the clock
doesn't tick, where the body is unlocked from pain,
where the wood thrush sings again after the rain.

HAND, HANDLE, LATCH

We come back to the window, again, again. The moon
climbs ivory, peach, chrome yellow, and buttons
up the darkening blue sky over the valley. We lie down
and a line of sweat sews a seam, my wrist to your back.

No sleep, no sleep. Fear opens a door, some moment you
are gone from beside me. Chris told me the story at work:

One morning she stepped out her door in the country,
and feathers fumbled all over her yard—bronze, brown,
black, red—and the small limp bodies plucked
by fox, raccoon, coyote-dogs. A child had left
the gate open. I see that gap, no more than a breath.

I reach out to pull the gate closed. Hand, handle, latch.
Lock against whatever hides and waits to come into our room.

THROUGH THE GRAVEYARD

Now we are half-way through the long fall.
Some leaves, those flakes of fire, smolder
under our feet as we take our afternoon walk.

Through the graveyard we talk about panorama,
perspective. In the labyrinth of turns we prefer,
at each we have a choice, and at our back
a blue-black smoke of cloud is beautiful, whether
or not we are overtaken, going home to shelter.

10

HOURGLASS

All night the wind throws sleet against the glass
like the sand stinging our faces and hands, the day
the hurricane's tail-end lashed us at the beach.

Time tumbles us back and forth in its giant hourglass.

One night at the beginning you stood naked in the hall,
it was storming outside the window, lightning, hail.
You flicker into light, arriving before me, once, again.

Time rattles at our window, time trying to get in.

11

SAVED [VOICE] MESSAGES

The automated voice says twenty-one days to erase.
All of your calls are filed into some cyber drawer.

The one about the eagle, the ones about the snow,
the miners' strike, Mumia, student protests in Arizona.
The one when you say, *Don't mind that errand.*
Come home and get loved up. The one when you hope
the bus ride wasn't rough. You fold all your electro-
magnetic energy into the digital envelope and send
yourself to me. The last one when you sound so sick.

I hit save, save, save, but I can't save everything.
Today I have eleven messages of us travelling
through time together, when there is yet no end.

. . . the moment before someone says a word

FIRST PERSON, HERE

I am making faint parentheses with my feet
on the park's white surface of unfolded snow.

I am making a trail, first person here after dawn.
I am watching for what is here I can save.

Trillions of slight periods of snow are ellipsing,
eclipsing everything. But when I look down, I see
others here before me: squirrel, dog, human.

The first is never the first, what with evolution and
six million years of us making our mark
on whatever we can, on frozen water that will melt.

Now a trace of this walk is in you who are reading.
In your ear and memory, the nuthatch roughly peeping.

SIP

A broken twig has scribbled on the snow.
Knocked down from the linden, it's written
nothing beautiful. Jagged calligraph, scrabbled.

Dried sap, sapience. A day when death is
breath, dry, drier, dehydration, me holding
the water bottle to your mouth, one sip.

A footstep line on snowfall points to the dumpster.
Diagram of poverty, and no sign if the person caught
anything this time with the hook of his cane. I'm not
the only one out. Muffled young men run, *How late
are we, man?* No answer but staggered haste.

On every sidewalk three or four sets of feet, blurred,
walking to work, people wearing the chalky snow down
to wet dark surface, clearing the blackboard. Mrs. Meigs'
parsed sentence, line and slant relation between words.

But what about the slope where words slide into silence,
the snow falling again, the people with heads down,
walking uphill.

Among the snow boulders on this block before dawn,
one heavy-coated person walking in the road, a man
coughing, two children waiting for the school bus,
two houses with weatherstripping and no siding,
two with blue tarps and no roof, two *For Rent* signs.

On this street, workers are living behind what's left,
opulent façade of another century, the stained-glass
veneer of lavender, yellow, blue. Someone is up
in the subdivided houses, the black metal envelopes
of mailboxes counting two four eight apartments.

Four more houses boarded up, three empty and one,
dead last, has plywood nailed over the bottom windows.

But on the second floor, lights come on, someone is
up in the half-condemned house. The snow counts up
as talk-show pundits say, *Things are better!* Here
we see the bust after every boom that means our jobs
and lives are exploding, the dust settling like snow
on our shoulders, and like cement around our feet.

WASTE

Scavenging around for something to save me from death.
Inching along the street edge of snow, staring down at
crushed flattened gutter fragments. May be something there.

Picking up the plastic bag flopped by the trash can, something
inside. May be something to hold on to, put inside this poem.

BOOTS WITH CLEATS

Don't slip! says Holly, shoveling at the door.
Some people haven't cleared their walks.

One relation of poetry to action—my boots
with cleats that dig into the glazed ice,
new-fallen snow, old ice lying underneath,
and the crunch as I push forward. I feel
that motion in the soles of my muffled feet.

20

Today I am a perfectly balanced scale of measure,
a plastic bag in each hand, potatoes, bananas, six
cans of beans, a newspaper's headline indictment
as Army private spills the truth about U.S. war.

The sidewalk is bare with chunks of concrete rubble.
The melting ice has stuck its cold watery hand down
into the cracks and pulled up and dragged out what
is underneath until the surface breaks and crumbles.

So cold, the birds only quiver a feather when I walk by.
So cold, crystal hairs of ice fur the snow. At Dominick's
I'm in line with the neighbors to pay for food. Silence today.
No conversation but *Three ninety-nine. Have a good day.*

It's just me thinking about the moment before someone
says a word, whether blather, stagger, anger measure scatter,
gather—the moment before that shapes every word.

Knowledge, admonition, lessons. The uses of the dead.
Tongues of grass flick at my booted feet on this old road
furrowed between a rank and file of graves. Stone tongues,
civilian casualties in secret war reports, the entombed.

There is no afterlife except our after. Winter ice, the snow
burying the dead grass, the unmarked bodies, a potter's
field, vessels broken and forgot, so close to us. The Army
shoveling millions of words over what really happened.

Some of us with hoe and spade in the wreckage, unburying.

NO WALKING AWAY

Today my heart flinches away from loss.
The trees are all bones and bark, skeletons,
their distractingly beautiful flesh of leaves
fallen, gone. No comfort in the cold.
No way to walk away from ice and sorrow.

CEDAR, ARBOR VITAE

The broken hawk lurches across dangerous space
toward the cedar shade, into the dark-green
fingers, and then its pale breast and feathers seem
no more than a glimmer of snow about to melt
and fall to the ground, gone into blue shadow.

If you were dead, my life would be like this street,
beautiful and bare. No more flying toward you.

25

THAW

Ice is not the stem it's wrapped around.
Clothes are not the limbs trembling under.

Words are not the marks I make walking.
Words are the water-drops, frozen crystals
on the cedar fingertips waiting for thaw.

Words are *Ahhh, I can't do this anymore,*
shouted by the man walking past, against
the wind. I am the footprint in the snow
already half erased by the northwest wind.

And you, reading this, you are the thaw.

. . . no time to be afraid

MISTY

Now the sky comes down as rain, slow, slow, slow.
At night, buried under blankets, we hear time slush by,
and go back to sleep. Boots on in the morning, I find
raindrops hanging from twig and thorn, transparent eyes
seeing everything, or tiny eggs clustered in the succulent
hen-and-chicks. Everywhere water waits until surface
tension breaks and the yolk slips out. Or the humor oculi
weep, water-drops slip down the knife blades of grass
digging out of the dirt, here, where in the early day
you call to me from the window: *Misty. Everything's grey.*

The sun is pulling back the snow to show
what has been broken underneath—or saved.

The tulip-poplar pod dry-scaled as snakeskin.
A clutch of rocks, motionless for now, hatching
in a hollow of light. Its ruff of ice is melting
as I watch. But when is the instant of disappear?

The green leaf beneath grows more and more clear.
I look down into the hollow of earth, the now. I stand near.

I don't want life with you to end so I say:
We never took those dance lessons. The spin,
the dip. There'll always be something not
yet done. One more trip to see the Falls fall.

I dreamed you said: *Let's go over together,*
and I said: *But I would die.* Not you, not you
dying in the dream, not you. We had the talk
about ashes, named the north and south
rivers to be sprinkled with us like pollen,
specks to meet again in some thundercloud.

Our boom, zigzag, bloom. Can we go see the Falls?
You will smile at me in the thunder and I will
not yet be pouring you through my hands, chalky
bone dust disappearing into the mist, eternal
beautiful disembodied matter. Not yet. Not you.

NIAGARA FALLS

Rain came and folded up the snow, put it away
for the year, except some pillows in the corners.

Rain fell again with a crinkling sound, someone
wrapping flowers in cellophane, maybe pussy
willows, the blurred fur blooms like the slush,
blush of soap on the car windows, the carwash
I drove through, dead of winter, to hear water rush.

Yesterday the cracked, parched lips of frozen ground
parted to the thawing rain. Now, long fingers of rain
write in the dirt, silver lines in the furrowed fields.

Water ladders down river shoals and leaps
over those world-famous falls, trying to come
again, to be a different element. What-was is gone.

It can rise into clouds on fire. It can turn to lightning
and make the sky write. What-will-be is still our story.

Got no time to be afraid, says the balancing waitress,
bacon and eggs and four plates. We're eating breakfast
at the diner, you are talking and I begin this poem. You
are sicker. *More tests,* say the doctors. Nothing to hold
between me and your death but some words. As long as I
carry words around and write them down, you won't die.

As long as I write and write, the words will still   33
fall over us like a snow shower in May, the day we sat
in the car at Schiller Park, and watched the wind blow
snowflakes like dandelion fluff onto new green grass.

MISCIBLE

We drive home through snow like torn wet feathers
whirling and stuck on the windshield glass, tiny barbs
and beads of a brief life, water to ice and back again.

Not dirt to dirt, we say, speeding through snow, sun, rain,
through salt mist spun from truck wheels. *Water to water.*

And we will be linked, molecules drizzling down
as tree thumbs and fingers are opening up. They
will catch us, they will drop us, soluble, unsolved, undivided,
undone, miscible mystery, down into the ground.

My ear at the corner of your sleeping shoulder,
listening at a closed door for what is said behind.

Now your breath, rushed, hoarse. Your feet push
like a treadle machine, like you sewing as a girl,
the awkward fit. Now your breath like the huff when
you work the scanner, running its thin finger of light
across your face. Now if I can make another *like*,
another *as*, you will still have a breath. One more.

Another. You will still be with me somewhere
in these words where I am listening for you.

MOURNING CLOAK

No snow, no bloom, the world is brown,
tattered, nothing to read in the dead leaves.

Then sudden semaphoring wings flap
fast, right under my nose, a quick prism,
crimson, scalloped yellow, blue-eyed snap.

The book later says it's a *mourning cloak*,
folded all winter into bark, named as if
it grieves. But something wrapped in that
flimsy cloth survived a minus-twenty freeze
and now is lit on an oak trunk, ready to lick.

Ready to wade head-first into the spring sap
sweating sweetly through every wrinkled crack.

TALKING TO MYSELF

Habit is acting as if we'll have another day,
me pulling the sheet smooth so we can fold
ourselves naked together if we get to the end.

This morning the muck earth and one robin
means we've gotten to another spring. The robin
claw-deep in mud turns its head now and then
to a sound. Why so still? There's some bird chatter
down the street, then a gurgle, a warble in its throat.
The robin small-talking to itself, or to the other birds.

I'm talking to myself to go on. I pick up maple twigs,
the tiny bud vases, the little red mouths, tattered
pale tongues littering the ground. They talk back to
me as I hold in my hands their broken chatter.

THE GULLS' CRY

Overhead the gulls cry *How? How?* and, yes,
I know it's me making meaning in their voice.

They are not amazed at the maples overnight
twirling their red tassels in the wind, they are
not dismayed that grey clouds inundate the blue
future of the sky, it's me, only me, trying to
rejoice three days after snow vanished every-
where, from the ground, from these poems,
as nibs of grass green the brown, ready to begin
their story again. Even as I stand and look down
at the muddy ground, unable to imagine how
I will go on without you.

38

Now the current has us, now we are rushing
motionless on the couch. No matter how close
I clasp you, I can hear the edge, the water slips
silently over and explodes below in the loud mist.

The end close and closer. My little gestures
to block and shape time, useless. The morning
of clicking on lamps, one, two, three, to make
sunlight against the grey outside vagueness.

The night of my hand folding and unfolding caress
across your back until we sleep, until we deliquesce.

Water to water, every gesture lost in the torrent
that claims us, and these words all that's left
of my bending over you every morning, this
morning, my mouth on your mouth, the unspoken,
the farewell, the truth that nothing of us will be left
to know the other.

. . . your wavelength, my wave

THE TORNADO

You and I saw the storm coming up the valley.
It made a precipice and from there it fell on us.

At the storm edge, a couplet of wind fragments
side-by-side, inbound and outbound velocities,
tried to clasp each other. Then a whirl into oblivion,
the only evidence of existence a cloud of debris.

43

Beauty into nothingness. You say, *Let's step back
from the window*. You clasp my hand. What will be
left of us? Bits of sound and matter, exhorting
voices inside the whirlwind saying the end is not
destruction, saying two is not the answer, saying
revolution is bigger than both of us, revolution is
a science that infers the future presence of us.

RAIN WORDS

Every morning this walk, a habit now. The words
written down, one foot after another. The sodden white
petals turn brown, the tender pages disintegrate.

I walk on, I follow the present into the next word,
what might return after you are gone, return you to me
in the future, the moment before I go out the door.

The two of us together in the patter of rain. You
turn over so I can kiss you goodbye. You say to me,
Yes, leave the window open. The air smells so sweet.

Moss in the cracked asphalt, this city acre
an empty parking lot. Red and yellow catkins
curl like caterpillars in the pavement mire.

Along the property line, the landscaped arbor-
vitae hedge leans like old pasture fencing
sprung from bird-seed shit. In that gloom,
chipping sparrows drill their songs, hidden
workers building the morning edge of spring.

As I walk by James Square, a small breeze,
the smell of drying clothes from 455 rooms
of sick, injured, bed-riding people. The unseen
work of staying alive. Watching for some haze
pinking the maple trees, for the blood of sunrise.

MAGNIFIED

I bend over the cobbled verge, the used-for-nothing-
now edge, except to make the little glints, insignificant,
that catch my eye. The first flowers, smaller than this *s*.
Smaller than this word. Pink jaws, blue bowl, white
knives. And if I had my pocket lens to swivel out
and magnify what I could see, then I would see us:

46   Inside the quiet rooms you almost never leave now,
us bending over the table, touching the painted wooden
eggs you gave me last spring. The white-seed dots,
the crosshatched grass, gold and yellow. The out-
stretched bloom embossed on red, blue, yellow, green.

You and me rolling the spring back and forth in our hands.
The silver mist outside, the next day we can't see, inside.

THE INVISIBLE (TO US)

The bitter herbs of spring crushed in my hand.
Henbit, dandelion, and the sharp green smell.

Going down the hill: First, a washed pink wall
paired with a square of blue, aesthetics of distance.
Then, cheap blue tarp replaces unaffordable roof.

My pleasure is real, a pattern back of my eye.

And the contradiction is real, pattern behind
the pattern. Crosshatching, currents, water, wind.
The little hairs in the throat of the henbit.

Blue streaks against white, guiding the bee's five
eyes, simple, compound, so bee legs scrape off
the invisible (to us) dust of survival. Magnified,
fearsome, caught in the flower's ferocious jaws.

NATTER

The elm tree, hip deep in snow last month,
now thrashes, furiously performing a sonata
through every crook, foot and branching out.
Its twin dances in the glass tower opposite.
They have each other and the blue sky glint.

A sketching class fetches the view from deep
inside the *camera obscura* of their eyes: trees,
high-rise cranes, humans too small to matter,
the valley spread over their wide white paper.

In my palm notebook, I write over illegible
loneliness as I walk. At the foot of the elm,
I find its scarred shed skin, bits of fire-wood
left to rot. So lonely. But the leaves still natter.
Fell fire-words yet to gather. Words, another self.

SHINING

The first morning after your worst night I walk
out into a shining. Bristled whiskers of light
on the campion's cheek, the pupil of nectared dew
in a tulip's mascaraed eye—Yes, the visual
profusion, but what I feel—I hold the eager,
the tender, the fibered stalk of flower. In my hand,
its slight yearning. The way I stroke your side,
your flank, trying to brush pain off into the night.   49

THE MOON, READING

The moon looks in our bedroom window at us
sometimes. As I lie down beside you, she pulls
a silvery sheet over us, and then retreats
to her silent night-time reading, east to west.

Night after night that bright gaze moves over us
lying under the comfort of being watched over.

The round illuminated magnifying glass
in Mama's hands as she passed into dementia
and understood less and less, her anxious eyes
reading the same line over and over. The moon
that shone in my window when I was little and
supposed to have religion, so I knelt and prayed
to that light, because she looked back at me.

Everything earthly and imperfect changes
under the moon. In this moment beside you
I am perfectly happy, lying in the moon's light,
drifting slowly with you into illegible sleep.

THE PEACOCK FAN

Another day comes, sun, you can walk to the car.
At the zoo we watch a peacock unfurl its spiny,
prismatic fan. The quiver of feathers, the quillwork,
the vibration faster than any hand could fan desire.

I say, *Remember the feather fan you gave me?*
I folded and opened the vanes to peer over
at the stern handsome face you wait behind.

You watch the world come at you, toward you.
Then you give another look that's just for me.

The glint, the sun striking the peacock blue.

The peacock ore I saw behind museum glass,
the copper iron sulfide rock burning at high
temperatures, volcanic, igneous iridescence.

Light responding to the surface of a substance
responding to light. Your wavelength, my wave.

East along the line of apple trees on Hawley,
the skin of the petals translucent in the sun, early,
the body and arms of the trees gleaming through.

I come closer and press my nose into the blossoms,
the fragrance of your skin, faint sweet sweat, as if
salt and all the minerals of the earth are called
up into you and alchemized by you, breathing out
through every pore what you've lived, your love,
your chemistry, your history, the smell of your skin.

LICKED

The people we were, the people we are now.
The apple blossoms blown, flowers fallen, blight
biting into every leaf, skin scaling on the trunk
and branches, skeletal shadows on the walk
as I pass, grieving and loving this boney brittle
world that breaks and opens day after day, the bees
gnawing at the red-hearted rose-of-sharon, licked,
sticky all over from flower tongues, pollen bristle,
until it's hard to tell the flower from the bee,
the insect from the tree, me from you, you from me.

53

THE DAZZLE: AFTER RITSOS

The shine is always there but well-hidden.
Without the sun, who could see the sparkle?

This morning, in and out, in and out, a dazzle,
and suddenly it's late summer, blue chicory,
hawksweed, the spidery anne's lace, my hand
stretching out, and I can almost grasp the you
who played behind the projects in the fields
through miles of flowers, the you still roaming,
the gleam at the beginning and still in your eye.

. . . do not seek to remain

I am reading Marx in the Eastwood McDonald's.
Fleetwood Mac is singing . . . *Don't, stop, thinking about*
tomorrow. Marx is saying . . . *Do not seek to remain*

something formed by the past but . . . in the absolute
moment of becoming . . . The words are ripping up
the moment and I fall into a tomorrow without you.

No morning, no night, no sleeping, no waking, no
dawn on your shoulder, talking about what is
the present. How do I go on? The way yesterday

a tree shook its small crescents of seed? Angled
for planting, sickled for reaping, red in the blue sky.
The answer in things, not words. But I yearn

to talk to you without end about what makes
that beauty and what that beauty makes of us.

The habit of living taken away. The green chalked
with white dust, like grief, like death on the way
to the river. To lose a person like you who can say,
The eternal nature of changing matter, who longs
to go ahead to see who will be on earth in a year,
in a million years. The sun overthrows the cool,
the river struggles with the shoals and breathes out
the rapids. Breathes out, out, the river breathes in
so quietly I can't hear. To lose a person like you
who can say, *The terrible beauty*. If you were here
you'd see how the coal dust rimes the river edge
in black sand, you'd see the lump-lunged miners
drinking beer in the shade, panting for their breath.
The people who just drove up, their child runs down
to the worn shoals broad as a spillway, and says,
We can wade in the shallows. Or maybe, *shadows*.

Everything is in motion, the leaf shadows hurry.
Everything is in motion, here at Hargrove Shoals.
The wind begins to make its afternoon way down
the river. The child counts to see how many times.
Fifty-three times! There is no *before*, and no *after*.

Eternal nature of changing matter. The terrible beauty.

Habit—the key in the ignition, and no, maybe never,
thought about why what happens next. Turn down
and onto Almond Street, sun into shadow, under the over-
pass. Then the red light, and sun gnawing at my ear.

The comfort of habit, not psychological. The pileated
cackle every year in the old magnolia, rejoicing
the chambered seed-cone has opened, the plump lick.

What habit gives us, and when it fails. Tushabe says
there were two seasons, wet and dry. The farmers knew
time out of time when to plant until now. The drought,
the weather has changed its habit. Or something else
has changed the mind of the climate.
                                We were watching
Norma Rae yesterday, holding hands. The mill hands
reached out and turned each switch off. How hard to break
the habit of work, obedience not to machines, but
to those who own them. The hand reaching out to take its own,
bringing the fragment, the red seed, delicious to the mouth.

CUT OFF FROM THINGS OUTSIDE

The red veins bleeding in the green leaves.
The green veins in the white bones of grass.
In the mist a breath of sun, the sudden bee.

How we work, work, work. Not our nectar.
No death overcome that way. The hope for
a fleeting look, to be even briefly seen. The wave,
the road crew's hand, *You, go ahead, go on by me.*

CORRUGATED

In motion—toward what? At my feet, corrugated
bark the wrinkled tree shook off in last night's storm,
growing and dying, and next, the end to sparrows
pecking and chirping in its ramified shade.

A long way off. And tonight's meeting is on how
to get people back snatched by the state, we know
not where, except probably no trees grow there.

Us in the trees. The trees planted inside us.

THE RELATION BETWEEN WORDS
AND PEOPLE: AFTER RILKE

Locked inside, the maintenance guy says. Squirrels,
destroyed eight, ten, windows trying to get out.

I walk around the school in the grey, up to the grand
façade of learning, like a real estate photo, slick,
until I get up close. Then borders run to dandelions,
clover, mustard and pasture grass, and the hawk
that lives on the tower roof whimpers and mews
and dives through the awards party, the punch
cups, the cupcakes. She flies into a tree with claw
empty, and tongue still outraged. The poem as prey,
as blood luscious, elusive. The poem as the locked room.

THE USE OF WORDS

What's the use of words dropped between
us and the other? Hawksweed, flower, yellow.
Yellow, caution, warning. Camera, security, eye.

They are watching *us*. I might call out for
Harriet Tubman, someone else *the justice system*—

Injustice depends on who the *us* is. And the *other*.
Depends. From every word hangs a warning,
the wind-snapped blood-stained banner of history.

THE DIFFERENCE BETWEEN INSIDE
AND OUTSIDE

At dawn the sky is chrome yellow. We turn over,
we say to each other, *Yes, the storm is coming.*

Thunder, purple, white light, red. At the window
I listen for rain to make its room of sound. How
once under the trailer-roof clatter, I was reading
about the future. Once I was under a tin-roof porch,
spatter, writing the spider lilies. Now rain spouts
like a turned-on faucet, I'm back in bed, the light-
ning strikes next door. You hold me, you say, *I've
got you*, petting my arm. You quiver into sleep,
my company inside the storm that's fading east.
A last thunder, inside me. My mouth wants to answer.

Outside I look for charred strikes, the long streaks
scorched down a tree trunk. The wind shakes rain
from the leaves onto a drenched length of cardboard
someone slept on, in the little room under the tree.

The slick wet surface of paper. In sleep your fingers
trembled. The dream when you made rally placards.
People were massing. What you had the strength to do
in your dream. Today the cardboard is unfolded
under the tree in the sun. Maybe the person sleeping
was alone, or maybe two lay in each other's arms
during the storm of night, wrapped in streaks of light.

THE NOW-RUNNING ELEVATOR

Not a word from inside or out in the early sun
graveyard. I'm just another body here, want to
find a line to start building on. I keep hearing the
repairman in the now-running elevator: *The bearing
burnt out, cut a groove in the sheave, boss wouldn't
let us blay-weld, so a 500-pound piece, we humped it
up the stairs last night.* He meant to floor fifteen.

V. Voloshinov (M. Bakhtin) said, *Language is
a place of class struggle.* For the living. That's me,
and you, if you are reading this anywhere, today.

THE CABBAGE BUTTERFLY

The human brain wants to complete—

The poem too easy? Bored. The poem too hard?
Angry. What's this one about? Around the block
the easy summer weather, the picture-puff clouds
adrift in the blue sky that's no paint-by-numbers.

In the corner garden, the cabbage butterfly
bothers the big leafy heads, trying to complete
its life cycle by hatching a horned monster to
chew holes in the green cloth manufactured so
laboriously by seed germ from air, water,
light, dirt. There's no end to this, yes, no end.

Even when we want to stop, stop, stop! Even
when someone else calls us *monster*. Even when
we fear and hope that we will not have the final
word—

There is a glittering spittle of dew on the green grass today
left by no human mouth, no human presence. It is work
done by the many-tongued world. I can only work

as nature does, *by changing the form of matter.* The necessity
of the human hand. I am writing a natural history of my world
with my two hands. Some of our work, done in this age.

Of course we wonder about our dreams, how they come from,
what they mean. Last night I worked in a warehouse, at a printing press,
and in the day room at break, the woman across smiled and said: *I'm
a communist.* Outside there was a huge shouting, one word, then another.

In between, a silent intake of breath, the moment between waves when
the ocean draws back to smash forward again. The sound was outside me
and inside me, and I was glad.
                                   Earlier I walked on Hawley Street
past a green lot, vacant, its one tree cut down, the trunk piled in pieces,
the mutilated branches sprouting leaves like fingers spreading even in death.

I woke, and told you the dream, and you said, *When the history of the world
is written,* and you meant, *By us.* The woman, the ocean, you, me. That *us.*

. . . now cast your shadow on my hand

The garden plot grubbed down to dirt since yesterday.
A blankness where there was—what? I can't remember.
The might-have-been plants, amaranth to zinnia, erased.

A half-eaten tomato on the bench, like a torn and bitten
four-chambered heart. Devouring time, I am not done
yet. Not yet. I'm writing down what you are doing to us.

THE LAST CONTRACT

Two pennies to weigh down the eyelids of the dead.
A penny on the tongue to spit out payment at the ferry.

A penny for your thoughts. Mine happen to be we need
money to cross over. At death's muddy bank, we pay.

At the big table we sat and signed the funeral contract.

The turn-us-into-ashes, the narrow profit-making door
will slide up or to one side. The fiery mouth opens
and takes us and coughs us back out in dust and bone.

The last contract burns up, and we become the something
that will make nothing ever again for money or for profit,
matter scattering, free to love in fire, in air, in dirt, in water.

Except. Water over the dam. Cents per kilowatt power.
Electric company towers marching, and no escape into death.

I'm on a path down to the river. In my eyes, another future
branching from this now. In my mouth, words, not money.

I'm watching rain fall out of green mouths, rolling off the tongues of leaves,
beaded and tasted like silver nonpareils, dropping dissolved to the ground.

I'm studying the use of leaves, the way they spit and spatter water,
the way our tongues lick words, shaping, re-shaping volume, duration,
   sound.

That steady trickle of sound, could be pleasure, could be pain. Could be
   anger.

EATING MULBERRIES FOR BREAKFAST

The trash tree, the splatters underneath like bird shit.
Like paint, like ink. The stained skin, dyed hand, pen.
Hand, thumb and forefinger, stub and nub of the matter.

Seed nubble, rubble, rabble on the tongue, drupe stone-
fruit. Flower-head so small, now root. Now splinter,
and shatter ground. Now cast your shadow on my hand.

74

SLEEVE

I lie in the dark, listening to a pulse of sound,
letters in an unknown alphabet spelling out words
that come and go through a sorrowful labyrinth.

And out of the corner of my eye, I glimpse you
passing down the dim-lit hallway, the edge of you.
Your sleeve, perhaps.

CLOTHED

The treading, the treadle of work, the going back
and forth between what-is and what-could-be. Me
trying to keep up. Before dawn, but warmer today,
and rainy, so this poem's coat is mottled and splotched
as first light shows through its thin cover. Pulling that
over you, as you say from your sleep, *Go out and live.*

I go, I leave you inside your pain-brocaded skin,
the skin draped in sweat. Every morning you wake up
clothed in pain. At night there's no taking that off
to put on a sleeve of poetry, no buttoning you up safe
with one more murmured word. That won't work.

DROUGHT

The green is growing and dying along the walk.
Grass-mown hay, and the clover-bloom debris,
handful of perfume, broken in my hand.

When I get home, you folded up, bent on the couch.
Harder and harder to get up. The graph of your decline
written onto the years we've held each other.

When I leave you and come into my room, the floor
is held together by braided coils of some unknown
person's work. The books are shriveling on the shelves.

THE YELLOW PILLOW

Inside the room is always the same: loss,
loneliness. The scene shifts outside the room.

Outside, outside. The only comfort inside
is the yellow pillow on the burnt orange chair.

My eye wanders, returns to its bright stare,
the shape of a sunny window but opaque.

A promise, always almost about to begin,
about to open, but then no begin. Only break,
only end.

LAST WORD

Now I am walking inside the apartment,
back and forth, back and forth, the end
is the beginning, the beginning the end.

You are dying. I write down your words
as fast as I can. They become visible,
electric impulse. What if you can never
change a word in that sentence again?
I bring you a damp washrag, other things.

No thing is like any other thing.
No word is like any other word.
There is no other you. The leaving,
the bereft word. Between us nothing
but gesture, back, forth, back, forth.

Other people go in and out the door, in
and out, down the hall, the smudged rug,
sit on the bench by the elevator, up, down.

There is no way out to where I want to go
with you. No word that will carry us out
together.

WAITING FOR THE FERRY

There's a place where the road drops
down to the river. People waited there
for the ferry once, for someone to come.

Now we're going down together.
At night, the trees are all darker shades,
the night sky makes the river silver.

80

You've never seen that road. I've never
made this crossing. The limestone shoals
stick up in the water, sharp as your bones
under your skin. You need me to help you
stand up or sit in smaller and smaller
places. The bed no bigger than a rowboat.

. . . flakes, flesh, flash

NOT FINISHED

The drops of rain wait in the yellow
tulip-poplar leaf. Fallen but not yet gone.

Waiting in the hollow, waiting for the sun
on the dried-up surface. Not falling down.

Waiting to be gathered up into larger,
into speckled scattered flecks of matter.

Flakes, flesh, flash. Something not finished.

DOWNSTREAM

Back on this side now. For now. Then was
night, heat. The streetlights streaked the floor
to an oily sheen. I brought you glass after glass,
the water you couldn't drink. It was the sixth week.
You were dying every time I lay down by you.

I said, the bed's our boat, we'll tie up under green
willow leaves and watch the water shadows.
But the river was drying up, down to a bed of rocks.

I could see some fish hiding, panting in the shallows,
lying downstream near a junked tire rim. I could see
the other side of the crossing come close to us, closer.

After months, after almost-death, after almost
nothing left of life-before, I get to the corner garden,
and on a bench there's a shattered shell gnawed
to pieces, a black walnut in green husks, unhoused,
its valves halved and hollow where the nutmeat
once grew sweet. Bees are bumbling in the borage,
yes, like that, all in the blue, as the cloud shadows
pass over the broken particles on the blue bench.

The wind shadows still pass over the river and
over its stone-tooth rapids at the ferry crossing,
even when I'm not there. I say, *Memory, come
in. Come in, river.* No, I'm not happy. No,
I'm not hopeful. For myself, I can't see where to go.

But the sun, equinoctial and even-handed, leans down
on my side. The wind also, and the wind shadows.

FIELD OF VISION TEST

Center, periphery, sparkles I set my eyes to catch.

On my scrim of memory, we move again, drive miles
to the darkest spot and lie down in the cold. The sky
wrinkles as we look up and see fiery tears in the night.

We let the stars fall down on us for hours. The fire
in us leaps up to meet debris disintegrated into light.

Smoke trails, swarms of meteors, bee flights of light.
In our eyes' oblique sight, that after-image lingers.

The destroyed glory, the speckled dust of the universe still
falls on us as the implacable day advances ray by ray.

THE PANTHER'S CAVE

Silence grinds me inside its big mouth, me
scrambling not to fall into the open grave.

Nothing I do or say will keep you and me
from sliding into oblivion. Death smooths
time like dirt over us, fills our ears. One
last word. Silence shoves and pushes you,
your breaths, me listening as the rain tries
to get in through the window to dissolve us.

What I hear is behind me: I am kneeling alone
in the panther's cave, facing the dead-end dirt,
and behind me, outside, spring water gathers
in the basin of tree roots, the water clear down
to each grain of sand, to each rotting leaf.

The trickle ticks downhill to the river now,
even now, when I can no longer hear the water.

WHAT IS LEFT

Now the days are going like cut grass,
the hay scent as I walk, clumps of mowed grass
dying, that sweet smell of the past
taken in my hand, the cool, the green of life
still lingering against my palm and fingers.

The little stripéd grasshoppers cling
to the curved blade of what is left.

THE BREATH OF THE DEAD

Another first snow. We see it together.

Your sweat and fever, iced down last summer,
sublimate and return in mist and frozen breath.

The crowded dead wait and gape in winter
at cold water's edge to cross into oblivion.

I thought I'd see you in that multitude.
Their breath in the snow, their oh-h-h's.

Wind drags the voices of the dead, howling,
over the metal window ledge, the harmonica
of what's left unsaid. What's the use of poetry?
Not one word comes back to talk me out of pain.

I go out to hear the music, and there is nothing
until almost the end. Then the giant drumming feet
as night escapes in cool flight, and then, the blaze,
the brass, the sun comes back. The only eye stares
back into mine. A voice, mine, is saying: *I stayed
to the very end. The very end.* That I remember.

What is left to say? In the end, you died.
And with your last mouthful of breath
you carried away the person you had been,
you took away the person I was with you.

At the end, you said, *This time I know I
am going, and you are staying.* But someone
unknown to me was the one who survived,
saying, *If only, if only we were still alive.*

THE FORWARD

How we have to go over and over things. Repeat,
beaten path. Repeat to bury, or uncover. The same
story told to the same person, again, again, again.

Yet another of these poems about death. Yes.
Again. Survival by repetition. The effort behind
the smell of cut grass, the swing back, the push.

The criss-cross of dying blades. You and me
lying down on the grass after that long hot march,
hand in hand on the cool ground, and then, pain,
our muscles seized to the bone. We almost can't
get up, but we do. Pain, and the body's memory.
The going-on of all the other marches. The forward.

AT THE BEGINNING

At the beginning, when you were sick,
we stood at the edge of the vast escarpment,
the sudden drop-off toward what we did not know.

The snow on our faces, the snow crystallizing
out of nothing as it met us and the granite plinth,
hitting our eyes and mouths, ice clouds slipping
through our fingers, melting from present into past.

And yet. The hope we took in that cold view cast
far beyond us.

ACKNOWLEDGMENTS

These poems were written for my beloved Leslie Feinberg, revolutionary communist and trans activist, theoretician, and historian. Details of hir life and work can be found at workers.org/2014/11/16937/ and lesliefeinberg.net/.

Grateful thanks to Suzanna Tamminen of Wesleyan University Press for her insightful and deft editing, and for the pleasure of our collaborative work; and also to Jim Schley for his thoughtful assistance in bringing these poems to the page.

Many thanks to Becca Shaw Glaser and Krista Kennedy for their early comments on the poems; to the Radical Education Collective workshop—Vani Kannan, Montiniquë McEachern, Yanira Rodriguez, and others—for their evenings of practice; to Rick Barber, Lyn Neeley, and Nick Orth for their later thoughts on the title; and to Don Mee Choi, Julie Enszer, and Marilyn Hacker for their encouragement.

Appreciative acknowledgment to the work of editors at the *American Academy of Poets / Poem-a-Day, American Poetry Review, Beloit Poetry Journal, Feminist Studies, Glitter Tongue, Heartland, Lavender Review, Literary Hub: Writers Resist, Poem: International English Language Quarterly, Poet Lore, Poetry Northwest, Prairie Schooner, The Progressive,* and *Sinister Wisdom,* where some of these poems were first published.

INDEX

Writer-activist Minnie Bruce Pratt's nine books of poetry and creative nonfiction include *Crime Against Nature*, chosen for the Lamont Poetry Selection of the Academy of American Poets, the American Library Association Gay and Lesbian Book Award for Literature, and as a *New York Times* Notable Book. With poets Chrystos and Audre Lorde, she received the Lillian Hellman-Dashiell Hammett Award from the Fund for Free Expression, for "writers who have been victimized by political persecution . . . as targets of right-wing and fundamentalist forces." She received a Lambda Literary Award for *The Dirt She Ate: Selected and New Poems*, and the Publishing Triangle's Audre Lorde Award for Lesbian Poetry for *Inside the Money Machine*. With activists Barbara Smith and Elly Bulkin, she co-authored *Yours in Struggle: Three Feminist Perspectives on Anti-Semitism and Racism*. Pratt, a managing editor of *Workers World/ Mundo Obrero* newspaper, lives in Alabama and central New York.

More information on her work is available at www.minniebrucepratt.net/.